Body

Moves

poems by Tim Seibles

CORONA
Publishing
Company

San Antonio
1988

Library of Congress Catalog Card No. 88-70160
ISBN 0-931722-68-3

Cover art by Brian Carlson.
Cover design by Betsy Davis.
Printed and bound in the United States of America.

*"What does what it should do needs nothing more.
The body moves, though slowly, toward desire.
We come to something without knowing why."*

Theodore Roethke

CONTENTS

Some of these poems have previously appeared in Blaze ("Satin Robes"), Dallas Studio Magazine ("Balance" under the title "The Soldiers"; "Light", "The Future", "The Leap", "To The World from a Restaurant"), Mundus Artium ("Hope", "Stranger", The Snail"), Sands ("Neverland", "The Place"), The Southwest Review ("The Ring Around the Moon"), The Sun ("The Body Knew"), Bloomsbury Review ("Big Mouth"), Black American Literature Forum ("The Word").

The asterisk is used to indicate a place where a stanza has been broken up by pagination.

BIG MOUTH

A few nights ago
you slept
with your mouth open
and the moon
slipped inside

because you have
such a big mouth
and now
your eyes glow
like a jack-o-lantern's.
Now

every evening
when you look out
the sparrows rally
and the plants lean
toward you
as though sensing
another dawn.

Don't try to explain. Imagine
even tonight, the trillion eyes
left heavy and moonless. Don't
look at me. You slept
with your big mouth
open
thinking you had
every right
and the moon snuck inside.

Already
the broken sky
has started chewing on stars
and soon the night
will be dressed
like a widow.

Don't say anything. Don't
apologize. Don't think
of all the lovers
by an otherwise moonlit lake
fondling each other
clumsily in the blackness
getting nowhere
because of you and your
big mouth.

Be glad
that your head glows. Be glad
that you'll never
need a flashlight
if your car dies
on a country road. You
slept with your mouth
open, open

like the bell of a tuba
only bigger   much bigger
and the moon
just couldn't
resist   so be happy
for that inner light. Be happy
and shut-up   shut-up
shut-up.

YOURSELF

It is morning.
Your eyes are lit like candles.
Throwing the covers off
you say to yourself
It is already tomorrow.

On the kitchen table
there is a loaf of blue bread
and a bowl of blue fruit.
In the china closet boats
of blown glass turn and twinkle.

You wonder who put them there.
You ask yourself *What clothes
should I wear.* You hope
someone will call and tell you
it's Saturday.

When the refrigerator clicks on
you don't notice. You are eating
the blue breakfast and trying
to sing. Blue crumbs
speckle the floor.

On the couch there is
a woman you always remember.
Her arms have become so long
that you think you need
to go to the bathroom

and when you open the door
you see yourself in the blue mirror
as though against the sky
and such a banquet of delusion follows
you don't see anything at all.

9

A MOMENT

It's Sunday afternoon
and Monday already seems
unavoidable.
Your eyes drift
like withered gulls
looking for a place to land
just for a moment
a moment as long and perfect
as the legs of a dancer.

When you lean back
your brain slides
to the back of your skull
like a baby pig
in a bowl of mud.
You're almost gone.
You want to tell the world
to kiss your ass

but somewhere in the house
a phone keeps ringing, room after room
you grog about picking up each receiver
saying hello, sounding polite—
you know exactly who it is. The voice
at the other end says *Hey, what's
all this about telephones? Lie down.
Get some sleep.* You stagger

to the next phone. Sleep
rides your back like a huge
retarded bear whose fur and
damp, friendly breath smell
like a grassy knoll in the quiet shade
of an old cedar in the undiscovered
middle of a forest

where you'd love to lie down
to whisper to the buttercups—
just for a moment
a moment as long and perfect
as the legs of a cheetah
upon whose back you would ride
from the city, through the country
beyond this Monday

into the heart of sleep

THE LEAP

It's morning. Your mind
leaps like a man with
his ass on fire. You're
late for work. It is
your ass. The boss is already
polishing the paddle. You hate

the pitying eyes of others
watching you approach his door.
You ask yourself *Will God be
like this*—big blood-shot eyes
orthopedic shoes, blockhead
bowed and slowly shaking
as though you were simply
some sad bastard come too late
to repent. You open The Door.

It *is* God, but she's beautiful
and relaxed, wearing a tight black dress
sipping Manischewitz. There are
your good friends. There are
your parents. There's Perrier on ice.
God smiles and opens Her arms.
You're stunned. You point to yourself.
A music falls over you like a fleece.

You're holding God's hand and
touching God's hair. Her arm encircles
your waist and suddenly you taste
the holy lips—you smack yourself and
straighten up, but God says, "Don't be shy"
and fingers your ear. You

don't know what to do.
Your father grins, "That's God, son.
It's alright." You feel so
good so many places with
so little effort—and to think
you were an agnostic.

After finding such a buddy
you will never work again and you
will not pretend you're Moses.
You will simply live
as though your brain were made
of a hundred drunken fish.
It's morning.

It will always be morning.

WHO KNOWS
(a chant)

There is a self in the middle of yourself
That knows that it knows that it knows it knows

What more can be said   what else can be told
There is a self in the middle of yourself
That knows that it knows that it knows it knows

How much of you is dead   how much has been sold
There is a place in the middle of the middle
That knows that it knows that it knows what goes

Who burned your bread and broke your fiddle
There is an eye between the eyes
That knows that it knows but it never shows

Who owns the world and gives you little
There is a weed in the middle of yourself
That knows that it knows that it knows it grows

Which root runs too deep   what sleep eats your nose
There is a stream way down in the valley
That knows that it knows that it knows it flows

Who sails your ship while you work the galley
There is a wind in the middle of yourself
That knows that it knows that it knows it blows

How much of you is covered   how much is unclothed
There is a moon in the blackest black black
That knows that it knows that it knows it glows

There is a self   underneath yourself
That knows   that it knows   that it knows

TO THE WORLD FROM A RESTAURANT

I'm a sad man at McDonald's. Let me
finish my fries. I love them—
it's late afternoon.
There are people all over who love Farrah's eyes
There are men who have walked on the moon.

In Rome a Polish Pope is prancing. He knows
he'll never be a groom.
The Lord says he doesn't need romancing—
that highest life starts in the tomb.

I'm just a man at McDonald's
with two tears to my name. I've come here
with friends and alone. It's *the reason why*
women must cover their breasts
that sets me so gently insane.

I dream, sometimes, of just going away
to the land where the sun drops its skirt.
I'd have lovers, good books, free time and sweet friends
and I'd finger my name in the dirt.

But I'm here at McDonald's—
let me eat my damn fries.
There's nothing but eating to do.
I grimace most mornings, but finally rise.
My cornflakes turn always to goo.

In Jerusalem the people must pray to The Wall.
We might as well worship one too.
There are people all over with fear in their eyes.
There are lizards that drink up the dew.

I'm a sad one at McDonald's—
there are others outside. They've
probably been here before.
I'm a man at McDonald's
with just two or three fries—
by now, I should own the damn store.

THE SNAIL

Sisters,
I am weak of your kisses
the wanting of them
the scheming for them, even now
with the sun out, even now
as I say it, even now
while the world warms in the sky's wide mouth
I am broken
for the lack of kisses, I am bereaved
of all the tongues shut away
in the black moonlessness behind teeth
behind smiles behind faces bruised
with unspent desire—what are we doing
so far apart? How many times has evening come in
like a woman and found me
kissless as a snail? How many hours
have I bullied the silence
talking about lips about the way a good kiss
spills into every untouched crevice
of the brain, talking
till my own ears bled of the words
and the sun rose again only to find
me, the same mad snail, talking
through the frost on my window
to the nubby grass, to the squirrels
the paperboy, to all of America, talking
about the wasted night and the nights
that will be wasted
while I'm drowning in the kisses
the way everyone is drowning
in that hot river of kisses
never tasted never tried.

JOSÉ

José, your breath is bad
from too much desperate talk
and your rabid hunger for women.
There are so many other things to do
besides this ranting of justice
besides this tireless dreaming
of your tongue being lost
in the wet and beautiful mouth
of some lady. Listen to me, José
that the mobs of imbeciles
are forming committees against you
that the private parts of women
sing to you in the voices of sirens
call to you with a sound as clear
and everpresent as air—
these are only bits of your madness.

Maybe America *is* a shark in the world
and maybe if you keep talking
you will find yourself
mushed in her great white teeth.
It would be just as well for you—
always squirming in your strange, invisible pain
like a little snake on a fork. Take off
those sunglasses. It is just as I thought:
your eyes are limp and shiny as though
you've been screwing every woman who passes.
Look at me, José. You are forever

burning and sinking like a bombed ship
over what goes wrong in the world.
You think the wealthy do nothing but
shit on poetry and make war for profit.
The way you yell and beat your fists—

.

it's as if your brain were a colony of ants
forever being ravaged by the long and sticky
tongues of the rich. You are not so helpless.
You are only frightened and long overdue
for romance, but this talking, this

moaning all night until
the moon crows and sags on its perch
and all this licking your lips
each time a woman touches a button
on her blouse—
José, if a woman ever smiled at you
there could be no stick big enough
to subdue that beast in your pants. You
would have to be shot.
It might be the best for you too—
always petting it with one hand
and pleading with the other. I
have never seen a hand so
eloquent with need. Of course

it is hard to understand the President
with his candle lit for Poland and now
not even a match for South Africa. I know Russia
is cruel, but what can we do with the Super-powers?
José, I forgive your politics—sometimes rage

is all we have, and a good lover
is the only country—but every dress
is not a dream, my brother. You can't
go on like this. My relatives
don't even ask about you anymore.
Put the glasses back on, José. The sun
is barely risen to the east. I
would hate for the sight of your mad eyes
to drive it off.

THE PLACE

Having been small once
I think it is too much to ask
for *maturity* with its

one dumb face. The moments
drift like balloons. People forget
and fly after them. Friends

change or die.
When I was seven
I saw the mornings

the sun drawing the dew
back into the sky, the asters hoisting
their big heads. Now light collects

like dust in my eyes. The dollars
are balloons. Something
living through

different faces
always takes my hands.
There is a place

so far away
I shouldn't even think about it
and a city of glass

clear as an embryo's mind.
By this time tomorrow
maybe we'll live there.

POEM

In Ethiopia
the candles are
going out
the children are leaving
just as they arrive—
enchanted   empty
the sunlight washing
their open eyes
to stone
while somewhere
under the same star
America
drifts toward
remembering
a debt—
the slave ships   the
slaughter
but now it is
nearly December
Santa
eats the mind
already and sooner
than we think
memory will have been
a small bite
Christmas is coming
with her twelve
children each
with seven maids each
with a candle each
with five gold rings
each
with a dish
of ice cream
and Africa.

THE WORD 1964-1981

In Philadelphia
I went back to the school
we integrated. The bunch of us
had no idea how big a deal it was—
our parents behind us saying
Be good now. Stay outta trouble.
But we were fourth-graders
and the teachers didn't want us.
What could we do? I became the class clown
Clyde grew the brain, and Reggie wore fake ties
all year round. None of us got A's.

Meanwhile "For Sale" signs sprang up
like tombstones. The cautious parents
were getting their young lilies
to the suburbs. There's not
a white face anywhere in the area now
except the principal who drives into the city
at dawn to lord over his black castle—
but the field is still there
and the bright yellow bases and
the twelve-foot fence I smashed into
leaping for a football. On
some of the side doors you
can still find the word *Nigger.*

TEACHING

Fluorescent light falls
like a fine snow
in the classrooms and
my eyes
fill up like empty
shoes

It is hard to tell
in this electric weather and
a lot of times I
just don't know
with the voices
gusting and the faces
of teenagers like flares
visible
for a moment
in the white darkness

Maybe I missed
the door to this season
I keep thinking
this wind
is real, this nervous
shuffling of hands and
feet, but I just

keep sitting here
and sweat
seeps from my skin
little by
little   the way
a soul bleeds
into a career
behind desks.

THE BODY KNEW

Long before there were words
long before there was *patience*
the body was twiddling its thumbs

Long before this haze of lies this
swirl of stupid things
said and done
the body knew

Long before the animals ran
from men before the lands
were named before the clouds
rose up and flew
the body knew

The body knew the tongue
would come up with something to say
that the ears would listen that
the words would come like ants
that soon the brain would be
infested and the head would grow
hard and heavy
The body knew the body

would be forgotten
The body knew the body
would be used to take the brain
there and there to make
money to make *relationships*
to assume the countless postures
of idiocy—to sign the contracts
and treaties to stock the stores
the homes the schools the offices
the streets the prisons the battle fields
the body-bags the body knew

it would be lost
under fabrics that soon the belly would
hang and the back would be stiff
that the days would pass the months would
pass the years would pass
The body knew

it would be rated "X"
because the body knew words
would be used to deceive to
decorate to pack the space between bodies until
reaching out meant climbing the mountains
of things said
The body knew

the brain would be a bully
that the face would be a canvas forever
painted with words that *love* could never be
what they said it was   that a word
was always a mask
The body knew the body

would dream of headlessness the way
a breast dreams of bra-lessness of blouselessness
of sunlight and weightlessness
The body knew that someday
it would have to move to forget to
dance to forget that it knew
what it knew
that it knew

BALANCE

When I
ask the soldiers
to be reasonable they
argue that
without a rifle
in one hand they'll
keep falling
to one side like
a man with one ear
made of lead like a man
with one lead nut like a
veteran with one leg
like an entire country
of misshapen men they'll keep
falling into each
other falling into the
earth they'll keep
rising like
the grass spring after
spring like a bombed
forest like a Dresden like a
burned man climbing
to his feet
as a bullet comes
to rest inside
his skull and
his brain
finally sings
in its broken
dish

CREOLE

With your lips like dawn
and your hair half-satin

bright sister, with your creamy body
whispering those liquid syllables, yeah

you with all that Europe
in your Africa. For you there is

a separate door in the air
and you keep gliding through it

over and over shutting me inside
the open corridor of your walking—

where did you get that rhythm?
My soul scats a new jazz. Near you

I am a dancing bear, tipsy
on the heavy brew
of my wishes.

SATIN ROBES
(for Anaïs Nin)

In the afternoon
when memories of the tongue's two sides
set your body afire

and thoughts that tug at your fly
hobgoble your sleepy brain like gnats

imagine a world
where the body is sacred

where only through touching
is the face of God revealed

the pleasure ghosting over the skin
like mist from a mountain lake

and remember your life   there
with the others   your heart adrift
its own deep waters   you

want to be cloaked
in the tongue's satin robes

so you kiss someone

and find yourself
warm inside a mouth
as you find yourself now

completely wrapped in air
your good body dissolving

hidden in cloth

SHUTTING UP
(to peacetime and prosperity)

It is hard to know when to say nothing
but right now seems like a good time—
why, with Venus sitting on a cusp of moon
and the federal cemetery kept like a garden
what keeps me wanting to talk about things?

It's not that I'm lonely. There are always
the others: my friends who pray to the bartender
my brothers, forever with one skinny reefer raised
and there are women I know who love so good
you never want to get dressed again.

I'm not so stupid anymore. I'm not looking
for myself—I'm right here—and sometimes
complaining about this life seems silly.
I live in a rich country: we have automobiles
and Coca-Cola. People here die by
natural causes. There is so much beef
I should be singing. Besides

my country knows what I need.
It says so on TV. It says *Be*
all that you can be and I've
always had wet dreams about the army
so I get my hair trimmed and wait for commands.
I end up with my friends who say
Friday nights are for dancing.

I put on my best pants. I ask them
do they dance because they feel happy. I
ask them are they happy because they are *hip*.
They say *Yeah and You know and C'mon!*
I can hardly remember the name of the place now

but the women there had tight pants and
tense blouses. They all had rhythm. They
were really in the groove. They wore
the new musks that let a woman smell like herself.
They were all what I needed

but I just couldn't choose—like all this night
with such a chance for quiet I just
couldn't shut up. Venus is gone.
The dark is over. A newspaper lands
with a slap against the door.

The dead soldiers are still married
to their hard blood and to stupid history.
I don't shut up, but I know it's about the same:
Venus will come back to purr in the moon's cool lap.
We will probably war again and my friends
my good friends and future lovers—
we will go dancing.

THE SHIFT

You come to know the lover
as a separate self inside you
a self that can't speak
but for moans—the naked spirit
powered fully by the engines
of the promise of sex.

Sometimes when you look up
even for an instant, and your eyes
come to someone you like
you can feel a shift inside
like the change in a crowd
when the pope strolls out.

This is the lover waking up.
This is the lover putting on its face
underneath your face. Your mouth
is suddenly wet, you take a deep
breath, a warm cloud blooms below
your heart. If you have ever

tried to resist you know
the walls of your skull
can never hold it because
at night in those dreams where
the midnight moon butters your lips
when your skin belongs

to someone's mouth and the tongue
opens you with its slick stroke—
this is the lover taking you back
to the first country
where the feelings are pure
and the whole self, clean and definite.

DOUBLE-DUTCH

In the afternoon tiny stars of sweat
beam from my skin, a mockingbird nabs
a bug, the seedy head of a dandelion
goes bald in wind and I'm starting
to remember an ice cream cone
I got one summer: I was up to my waist
in weeds. There were the weird berry trees
the red apartments and me
with a bucket full of grasshoppers.

In the alley down the hill three chocolate girls
two turning two ropes swaying, "3-6-9
the goose drank wine, the monkey-chew-tabacca
on the streetcar line" and the one in the middle
jumping double-dutch as though there were
no time and no other way. Later

I was going to the schoolyard. I was going
to play football with Melvin, Snooper
and Jimmy-White. They would be waiting
in the big shade by the monkey-bars, and maybe
Crystal and Vanessa still in t-shirts
with their "big stuff". Me and the fellas
would make dishonorable plans for the night—
I knew what Mel would say. I knew we itched
for those soft shapes under cotton. Then
my mother called me. She was across the street
holding an ice cream cone.

It was lemon.

THE KISS

José, do you remember the first kiss
you did with your mouth open?
But of course not, since you are
such a Godzilla, you will spend your life
waiting like a man whose bus never comes.
Anyway, when I was fifteen there was this girl
named Jane. Because of her, most of us
walked around with something like a rock
in our pants—and the neighborhood was struck
by an epidemic of wet dreams. Sometimes
they were hand-assisted, but still
it was Jane's fault: she always looked
like she needed to be kissed, not savagely
but hard enough to require Vaseline on the lips.

It was a bad time for me and my friends
at this small Lutheran school. There
were few girls and fewer still black girls.
In the public schools rumors of *fast pannies*
ran shining like sunlit satin down the halls—
stories of big-legged babes who would take on
maybe five lucky dudes at once!
At our scrawny-little, goodie-goodie school
we were enslaved by the prospect of a kiss
even a little smooch, not held for an instant.
A *hug* would have been worth big conversation.

Anyway, because Jane was so fine, I figured
trying for her would be useless—my hair
wouldn't grow and afros were big back then.
Back then, if you were dying in the street
without a big bush most girls would
just leave you for the buzzards—
and the guys who talked to Jane had afros so big
they looked like walking trees.

But, by some sweet scratch of luck, Jane
took my hopelessness for poise and hinted
that I should call her sometime. Of course
I wanted to seem cool, but, José
it was all I could do to keep my heart
from ripping my shirt. That night
my nervous words scrambling over the phone
I arranged to visit her. On Friday
with the moon out and a big mouse in my gut
I walked the eight blocks to Elm Street—
mouth dry, pulse stuttering, but every strand
of my measly hair oiled and perfect.

When she opened the door she looked
so good I had to squint or my eyes would have
wrestled her to the floor. There was music
and just enough light and water which
I needed badly—if the time came I didn't want her
to think my tongue was a dust-ball and pull away
disgusted. We sat on the couch listening
to The Delfonics, their voices weaving bells
into the air. My left hand crept

onto her shoulder. My breathing stopped—I
had to make a real move or be a chump forever:
I leaned over. I kissed her cheek. I waited
to be crushed like the desperate roach I was
but she said nothing and the slow music
kept falling over us. Then, possessed
by some perverse ghost, I dove into her ear.
José, I am surprised that her head isn't flooded
to this day—that ear! My tongue tracing
the crescent curve, then down to the bit of wax inside—
the top of my brain singed with the taste of it.

I could still be there now

if she hadn't led my lips to hers and
pulled me into the wet, warm wilderness
of her mouth: a tiny jungle, my brother
but one from which I am still climbing out.

THE FAN
(for Martina)

I'd love to tell you
that watching
a woman play tennis
isn't sexual
but when Martina serves
and her perfect body
uncoils like a whip from
the toes of her Pumas to
the forked tongue
of that cobra she calls
her left hand

my insides get all
hot and crowded
as though my heart
were a watermelon
filled with Augusts
so I have to
unbutton my shirt and
when she

volleys those volleys
those volleys she volleys
those wingless sparrows the opponents
send back to her—
her calves flashing her
satin-steel torso stretched
balanced fleeced with sweat that
Czechoslovakian face on fire   I

just can't stand it—my shirt
my pants coming off—her racket
coming to the ball coming
for one good kiss one taste of
heaven one hard bite for
pain for pleasure
the air opening
its invisible thighs: the shot

untouchable   unthinkable
almost holy
licking the line
licking the umpire who
called it good licking
the ball girl and
the oooing crowd and
me standing there in
boxer-shorts with my
eyes closed my head
thrown back screaming *Do it,*
Tina, do it!

LOOKING

Brothers,
I am sick of burning
for women, sick of saying
Look at her, look at her, Lord
have mercy. I am sick of this
ticklish ache, these body whispers, this pubic smoke
that creeps through my veins till my brain
is choking, sick the way a dog must
get sick of summer: tongue touching
the street, tail dragging, his balls
full of June. I am sick of wanting
the big legs of black women, of watching
them pass with those high, holy half-moons
of ass swimming side to side like round, finless fish.

I am sick of tight pants—
the way they ask to be pulled down the way
an orange begs to be peeled. I am sick of all forms
of bra-lessness, especially when the blouse is thin
and the nipples keep trying to peep through
like eyes fighting a blindfold, like delicate
bite-sized bulls charging gently through
a matador's cape. Of course, I am sick
of slit skirts and stockings: downtown
the women walking and with each step a flash
of thigh—a sly whisper of what sings
a little higher, the muffled chorus of lingerie
living in that eternal twilight above the knees
beneath dresses behind smiles. I am sick

of bearing this broken halo, sick of being
blown this way and that by the beautiful winds of women—
and the dancers too, even with their strong legs, their
rippling backs, their suggestive agility—I want none of it.
Not the velvet dark of a señorita's eyes either, nor
the silk forest of her hair, not even her tongue
made smooth and delicious by the constant rolling of r's.

Brothers, tell me nothing of the blue eyes, the curls
the ebony skin, the flowering of ankle into calf, of waistline
sloping into hips and thighs. Say nothing of the snugness
of snug shorts and nothing of the sweet, full lips
whose sexual wings beat the mind's thin air until even
the soul kneels and weeps. Don't mention the possible
paradise and all the paradise lost because I'm drowning
in this deep river of women. My lungs are filled with looking—
I am sick, sad and sorry I ever listened
when Puberty called.

WHAT HOLDS YOU

There are places in your body
that no music can possess. This
is not a good night for dancing.

Outside the wind pulls a wet comb
through the trees and mistletoe
spiders in the bare branches.

You feel an obsession coming on—
someone you can't do without.
Ever since sundown Thursday

something has been turning in your belly
like a gear in a watch. You can't help
but imagine the moon-glazed skin

inside her blouse and the invisible rising
of her breasts as she breathes.
Tell yourself *It's just a mood, it's*

only evening—it's January.
The temperature has been strange
but what holds you, what really

keeps you talking to yourself
is the smile, the lush pink
of her lips and her mouth

which must taste like rain.
This is the brain's favorite weather—
a possible lover looming

out of the city, her hands the color
of candlelight opening towards you, the night
gathering you like a wind in its heavy vines.

If she came to see you. If she wore
a silk jacket and nothing but the breeze
underneath—what clock could strike that hour?

It is late. You should sleep. You
have already called twice. New words
from new alphabets   are taking over

your life.

THE FUTURE

Close your eyes. You are
in a field. Your skin blossoms. You
begin the dance: one smooth step left—
one big hop right. Your breath
is the only music. You don't know
why you're going or where
you've been. You can't tell
where your body stops
and the sky begins so
you close your eyes.

It's almost noon. Two trees
have risen and a small singing
floats in the way a small light
comes from a face. One smooth step
left—one big hop right. You see
a bird. There is an argument.
An old man pedals by, his pale legs
spinning and spinning so you
close your eyes.

A basketball hoop films
with the cool gray air of dusk.
The swings are nearly invisible.
You are there in the schoolyard looking
for everyone else. High up, a woman
shining and black as a seal
leads the dark and the moon across the sky.

The future is yours: one
smooth step left—one big hop right.
You will dance all day. You will
dance all night.

THE PRAYER

First, say nothing
as the orange twilight pours
through the windows
and your body unfurls
its invisible banner, its sails windward
to the wind of the hands
of your darling.

Do not question
the easy lesson of moist lips
moving along your neck
just follow
that exquisite tickling
as you would a pretty sound
coming from someplace unseen—

where it stays summer
always early morning, always
the one flower giving up
its thin robe of dew.

Then, you must
give yourself completely
to pleasure
as though Pleasure were the country
of your birth and your allegiance
were unshakable, as though

every turn brought you back
to the garden of tongue tasting sweat
of saliva glistening on the lit tips
of breasts, of the long tropical kisses
between the legs, of fingers praising
the temple of flesh, touching each pore
as though each were the mouth
of a burning angel whose thirst
opens the way to the soul
turning   on the spine's porch.

And finally, when you've had
just enough of too much—
when your brain goes black
and you land in the river
east of death
where the current is your body
moving back to that perfect balance
that dreamless sleep of gods

you must remember
that certain sweep of color
through the air, that friendly look
in your lover's eyes
that holds the prayer:

say nothing.

WHO

Who doesn't
want to dance
to be inside the body
not somewhere beside it
to feel the arms and legs
hot and clean in a clear lake of air
like fins, as though every limb
were a fish for a moment
free of the water out of the world—
the body, strange as a planet
reeling in its own soft sparkle

Who doesn't want to dance
to let the body go gracefully mad
to fall into the music as though
from a cliff—every muscle a feather
every three feathers a bird every bird
bald blind and falling
as though the fall itself were the dance
as if the music were a cushion of air
a wind holding you up as though
in motion the body is a leaf is a
new fabric better than feathers better than water

Who doesn't want to remember the feet
to wash them in music
to feel gravity's tireless kiss
bringing you back, pulling you in
as if there were only you and the earth
and music were the sea
and the body were a small ship with lungs
as its sails—as though breathing
were dancing and dancing were living
and living were enough. Who
doesn't want to dance?

SWEET
(for C & P)

Looking into your eyes
is like opening a door
through which I find you
in a blue dress
by a window, the wind
ladling your hair
into my hands
as though your hair
were a dark stream lit
by the light a lake gathers
at night. Some memories

are so sweet
that they burn in the mouth.
Others, I would make
but the days, the husbands—
they keep leading you off.
I wish the world didn't ask us
to choose lovers one at a time.
I wish there was a moment
I could keep and a room
beyond this door in myself

where I would find you
free as the light a lake gathers
your eyes unworried
your goddamn hair in my hands
your body, your mouth
over here
with the world out of the way
some kisses—
not another time
this life
some kisses
over here.

45

THIRD WISH
(for W.H. Auden)

Sometimes some things are just hard to know
So often I think there's so much I've missed
But someday today will be long ago

I watch women walking, I watch children grow
This looking sends me such a fragile bliss
Sometimes some things are just hard to know

Down here the days fall like toy men in a row
I pay all my bills, I check off the list
But someday today will be long ago

I keep asking questions, but the questions don't know
When you whisper a prayer does it land like a kiss
Sometimes some things are just hard to know

I keep a straight face, I look calm even though
My parents never told me it would get like this
But someday today will be long ago

If I knew it I'd know it and I'd let it show
I walk through the world like each step's my third wish
Sometimes some things are just hard to know
But someday today will be long ago

THE RING AROUND THE MOON

About this time every summer night
my cousins would stake out the porch
and wait for the slugs to drift
sleepily over the planks like long ships.
In the drab light small hills of salt
glowed in their hands. Then

the slugs came, trailing their sticky footprints
that would be crystal by morning. Even
when the first were hit with salt and burning
the others kept on—no worried pace
no notice of the dying until some nights

the relentlessness of teenaged boys
left the porch ablaze with melting bodies
and pools of salt and the moon
around which thousands of the slim souls
turned and turned

NOTHING BUT FOOTBALL
(for Melvin Strand)

I

Brother, those days in the schoolyard
playing football with the sun
preaching heat to the asphalt, when
we thought everywhere was Sharpnack Street—
those were good days: you and me
and all the moves we used, our feet
fast and smart as God, our heads saved
from everything but dreams
of getting the ball and that single
glorious, ever-present possibility of *touchdown.*

II

Our sneaks laced with *NFL Highlights*
Mel, with a football in our hands we were
right as priests: celibate, heaven clearly in sight
ready to abandon the world just to get closer
just to fake the hell out of anyone
trying to stop us. They couldn't stop us—
You stutter-dipped, I snake-slipped, anything
to spin-shimmy away clean as light, slick as sweat
holy thieves in a forest of moving trees: What
hymn, what hidden but unquestionable singing
did we dance to then?

I hated to play against you, trying to read
the mystical sermons of your feet, the blur
of your Converse high-tops, that sudden cut that
always came sure as dark, you smooth bastard
and the finishing gallop that left us praying
to your back. There was nothing
more beautiful, no creature more purely one
with its escape, and I have loved nothing
and no one more than that twelfth summer
we roamed the schoolyard beyond our parents
riding a football into this life—every day
a new game. Every catch a blessing.
Every opening, a parting of the sea.

NEVERLAND

At the end
of those old hot-rod movies
after the poor kid
ruins the rich punk
in the quarter-mile drag
ignores the trophy
and putts smoothly into the hills
with the sweet Italian girl

you might picture him
forever finding shade by a pond
loving her till his ears ring, pressing
her sleek shape into the soft shore
then driving on to the next pond
and the next—the year
jammed at summer

so you travel along
inside yourself becoming him.
You like her kisses, the sunlit silver
of the shallowing fish
the roads always coming to water.

Back in the world
it can never be like this—
the good-guy wins and
wins, the eye within your head
opened wide, but not confused or desperate.
Her lips, your hands
the conversations
this neverland stumbling
from joy to joy.

SOME OF THEM

In South Africa
some of them wear their skins
like weapons   like pale blades

like gold   as though they
as a race had been lifted
from the darkness

lifted to rule
the sunlit air   to issue
commands like jewels
to the others   Once

upon a time   some of them
came to America   walking on water
with their wooden ships

walking on water with their
bright eyes   their bibles
like daggers   their veins green

as money beneath their translucent skins
and the Indians were amazed   said *Yes*
this is corn   Yes this long water
is called Mississippi   Yes
stay awhile   Eat with us

Right now   it is hard to say
what some of them
won't do If once if only
once

some of them would hesitate
smell the blood   smell the forests
but already the earth

is being remade   in their image
just ask the oceans   already the President

whose face is wax whose nose
is melting   has turned
his winsome grin
                    to the sky

THREADS AND FLEAS

Think about the first thought
and the first person
to have it—how scary
it must have been to feel
something uninvited taking shape
inside, how that first idea
must have glimmered
like a bug in the brain's dim kitchen.

Think of sundials, the shadows of days
rising and falling like wings
over the circle. Think of time
as a color too clear to see, like
that music you can almost remember. Think
of History's huge quilt, how somewhere
hidden in that enchanted weave of passion
and confusion is the one thread
that has you here   now.

Think of everybody. Think of all the threads
and questions drifting like
dust in the air. Think of the singleness
of being yourself thinking
of what everyone else
might think. Think

until your brain starts
to bake in its stone-walled oven
until every thought is a flea and
your brain is a dog's soft belly in summer.

Think until the fleas begin eating
each other and the tiny screams
all together sound like a kettle whistling
on the white stove of the skull.

Think of everyone thinking like this
of each mind rioting, each trapped
in its kitchen of bone sealed beneath some
steady face—in some room, on some street
somewhere in this country. Think of all the Americans
going to work, going to school, to lunch, to
sleep, just going with heads full
of fleas. Think of the centuries

flown like painted birds, like
wild, intricately woven dreams
lost in that sudden opening
of eyes. Think of Africa and Asia, of
India and Europe, of each person ever
born anywhere, and each death and
the cemeteries simmering
with the itchy dead—each
with a finger still scratching
on the locked galley door of the head. Think
of every thought found, kept or forgotten
on Earth

and think of *Earth*, all this time
an iridescent bug in the sky, in the Milky Way
in the ebullient, blue river
of endless space.

STRANGER
(for everyone who listens)

Sometimes the moon comes to me
so haggard that a pigeon
might brighten the sky as much.

A mist flavors the air.
A long kiss, a voice—nowhere
all gone as the eye that dreams.

I don't know what might save
my country. These are the nights
when the idiot makes a fire

and warms his hands till they blacken
when he yanks two bones from a bull's nose
and beats on a log.

Everybody comes out slightly unzipped
and smiling. The lights flicker.
The carpet is covered with shrimp.

Tonight I realize all this
is inside my face. If I keep my secret
I keep my job and steady pay.

If I rip off my clothes and start
drooling on everything *The Respectables*
will say I'm going mad.

I'm already mad. If it wasn't for you
I'd see a blade in every hand
and blood in every grin.

The moon is teething on stars.
It's January. I'm stranger
than I've ever been.

HOPE

Listen. Someone is dead.
The eyelids drop like two leaves
into the shallows of a pond. Listen.

The phone rings. A low voice
bleeds through the wire: the bad news
crowds everyone toward that one

last breath. Listen. We are
still breathing. All over the world the lips
keep shaping the words. Listen.

We are not dying—
the brain stays in its private room
spreading the map like a Caesar.

New cells chirp like toads
in the body's shallows. Listen.
It is this life that matters.

When we talk like this
with the night balding with the sun coming
with the everything breathing fire on us
I want to tell you that this *is* Eden.
Nothing has changed, no one was cast out.
The world has always harassed us:
if it isn't love it's mud and rust
in the brain; if it isn't the morning
come too soon it's the night
lingering like a stain in your eyes—
the insects, the germs, our jobs
eating us intently and this hard season
of aging separately no matter how we try
to hold on, and you, José, if you are not
enraged by the lack of kisses you are
snorting like a two-legged bull at America.

But there is less to it than this.
There is the cracked joy of being mortal
and knowing it, the knowing that
even as you set fire to yourself
again and again and come flying out
someday you will get a rest
that no war can interrupt.
So dream of an island made of lips
where every single step is a kiss
or worry yourself with missiles
and white presidents   the quiet
will come just the same. I know
you think I'm a weak, happy-eyed old dog
curling up with these days because
I'm afraid to fight, but sticking out
your mouth will do nothing now.
We are no longer children, my brother.
We must perfect our illusions.

COMPANION

If we could forget enough
we could get back
to the beginning of
ourselves   where
there is no such thing
as bitterness

where the mind moves
like wind through the world and God
is tangible as black earth and evening

If we could stop remembering
all of the names
History has thrown to us   we
could go out for awhile

and of course the sunlight
would be there waiting
would bounce off the grass off
the water off the tiny backs
of bees and onto our bellies

as though each body
were a soft mirror
so we'd all feel like shapes
of changing light like
little moons with hands
and feet shimmering

If we could just
forget to remember   right now
our lives would come back to us
like lost animals   finally
on a fast trot ears perked
to the voice
of a necessary companion

LIGHT
(for Fern)

It is easy to pray
when the moon is like this

Half your brain going dark
half the night over
the air lacing its silk sleeve
around you

On what other planet
could it be like this

I have come upon a woman
whose skin is golden
whose green eyes
bear a light

nothing like the moon's

THE DRAGON
(for Carlo)

José, I wasn't always bald.
It took many thousand beers
to make this stomach
and many thousand kisses
to chafe these lips. Maybe
I'm not so fast anymore and one
gentle woman can tire me out
for a week, but I'm smiling
and the ladies can walk past
beating the air as if to fly
with their mouthwatering parts
and I don't need to douse my head
in the brook. My brother, it is no sin

to be content, to love what lives
in our faces that makes the birds flee
and the strays come shyly to us.
But it can never be that I'm
only pleased—terrible things
will happen to us! Look at the cricket
hung in the web and the spider
in the beak of the cardinal
the bleeding men, the broken faces
and the soldiers who keep tonguing
their rifles. These are the teeth

of the dragon whose jagged breaths
tear through us like blades.
How much killing can a man see
before he dies from watching?
How much of what is big inside us
is dead from trying to come out?
But, José, it's alright—we are not
so easily beaten. There is the music
of guitar and your mad black face
to live for.

COMPANION

If we could forget enough
we could get back
to the beginning of
ourselves   where
there is no such thing
as bitterness

where the mind moves
like wind through the world and God
is tangible as black earth and evening

If we could stop remembering
all of the names
History has thrown to us   we
could go out for awhile

and of course the sunlight
would be there waiting
would bounce off the grass off
the water off the tiny backs
of bees and onto our bellies

as though each body
were a soft mirror
so we'd all feel like shapes
of changing light like
little moons with hands
and feet shimmering

If we could just
forget to remember   right now
our lives would come back to us
like lost animals   finally
on a fast trot ears perked
to the voice
of a necessary companion

LIGHT
(for Fern)

It is easy to pray
when the moon is like this

Half your brain going dark
half the night over
the air lacing its silk sleeve
around you

On what other planet
could it be like this

I have come upon a woman
whose skin is golden
whose green eyes
bear a light

nothing like the moon's

THE DRAGON
(for Carlo)

José, I wasn't always bald.
It took many thousand beers
to make this stomach
and many thousand kisses
to chafe these lips. Maybe
I'm not so fast anymore and one
gentle woman can tire me out
for a week, but I'm smiling
and the ladies can walk past
beating the air as if to fly
with their mouthwatering parts
and I don't need to douse my head
in the brook. My brother, it is no sin

to be content, to love what lives
in our faces that makes the birds flee
and the strays come shyly to us.
But it can never be that I'm
only pleased—terrible things
will happen to us! Look at the cricket
hung in the web and the spider
in the beak of the cardinal
the bleeding men, the broken faces
and the soldiers who keep tonguing
their rifles. These are the teeth

of the dragon whose jagged breaths
tear through us like blades.
How much killing can a man see
before he dies from watching?
How much of what is big inside us
is dead from trying to come out?
But, José, it's alright—we are not
so easily beaten. There is the music
of guitar and your mad black face
to live for.

59

When we talk like this
with the night balding with the sun coming
with the everything breathing fire on us
I want to tell you that this *is* Eden.
Nothing has changed, no one was cast out.
The world has always harassed us:
if it isn't love it's mud and rust
in the brain; if it isn't the morning
come too soon it's the night
lingering like a stain in your eyes—
the insects, the germs, our jobs
eating us intently and this hard season
of aging separately no matter how we try
to hold on, and you, José, if you are not
enraged by the lack of kisses you are
snorting like a two-legged bull at America.

But there is less to it than this.
There is the cracked joy of being mortal
and knowing it, the knowing that
even as you set fire to yourself
again and again and come flying out
someday you will get a rest
that no war can interrupt.
So dream of an island made of lips
where every single step is a kiss
or worry yourself with missiles
and white presidents   the quiet
will come just the same. I know
you think I'm a weak, happy-eyed old dog
curling up with these days because
I'm afraid to fight, but sticking out
your mouth will do nothing now.
We are no longer children, my brother.
We must perfect our illusions.

Eight Hundred and Fifty copies printed
May 1988